"A day without laughter is a day wasted."

- *Charlie Chaplin*

Copyright © 2016 by George Grokhowsky and William Merne

Visit us at: www.InternetJokeBooks.info

ISBN-13: 978-0-6928-6684-9
ISBN-10: 0-6928-6684-1

First published: April 15, 2017

# The Internet Joke Book

By: George Grokhowsky and William Merne

# Table of Contents

# Animals

## Bad Parrot

A young man named John received a parrot as a gift.

The parrot had a bad attitude and an even worse vocabulary. Every word out of the bird's mouth was rude, obnoxious and laced with profanity.

John tried and tried to change the bird's attitude by consistently saying only polite words, playing soft music and anything else he could think of to 'clean up' the bird's vocabulary. Finally, John was fed up and he yelled at the parrot. The parrot yelled back. John shook the parrot and the parrot got angrier and even ruder.

John, in desperation, threw up his hands, grabbed the bird, raced to his kitchen and put him in the freezer.

For a few minutes the parrot squawked and kicked and screamed. Then suddenly there was total quiet.

Not a peep was heard for over a minute.

Fearing that he'd hurt the parrot, John quickly opened the door to the freezer.

The parrot calmly stepped out onto John's outstretched arm and said, "I believe I may have offended you with my rude language and actions. I'm sincerely remorseful for my inappropriate transgressions and I fully intend to do everything I can to correct my rude and unforgivable behavior."

John was stunned at the change in the bird's attitude. As he was about to ask the parrot what had made such a dramatic change in his behavior, the bird spoke up, very softly, and asked, "May I ask what the turkey did?"

# Bear Remover

A man in northern Minnesota woke up one morning to find a bear on his roof.

He looked in the Yellow Pages, and sure enough, there was an ad for "Up North Bear Removers." He called the number listed and the Bear Remover said he'd be over within an hour.

He arrived, and got out of his van. He had a ladder, a baseball bat, a 12-gauge shotgun, and a mean looking, heavily scarred old pit bull.

"What are you going to do?" the homeowner asked.

"I'm going to put this ladder up against the roof, then I'm going to go up there, and knock the bear off the roof with this baseball bat.

When the bear falls off the roof, the pit bull is trained to grab his testicles, and not let go. The bear will then be subdued enough for me to put him in the cage in the back of the van."

He then handed the shotgun to the homeowner. "What's the shotgun for?" the homeowner asked.

"If the bear knocks me off the roof, you shoot the dog."

# Dead Duck

A woman brought a very limp duck to a Veterinary surgeon. As she laid her pet on the table, the vet pulled out his stethoscope and listened to the bird's chest.

After a moment or two, the vet shook his head and sadly said, "I'm sorry, your duck, Cuddles, has passed away."

The distressed woman wailed, "Are you sure?"

"Yes, I am sure. Your duck is dead," replied the Vet.

"How can you be so sure?" she protested. "I mean you haven't done any testing on him or anything. He might just be in a coma or something."

The Vet rolled his eyes, turned around and left the room.

He returned a few minutes later with a black Labrador retriever.

As the duck's owner looked on in amazement, the dog stood on his hind legs, put his front paws on the examination table and sniffed the duck from top to bottom. He then looked up at the Vet with sad eyes and shook his head.

The Vet patted the dog on the head and took it out of the room.

A few minutes later he returned with a cat. The cat jumped on the table and also delicately sniffed the bird from head to foot. The cat sat back on its haunches, shook its head, meowed softly and strolled out of the room.

The Vet looked at the woman and said, "I'm sorry, but as I said, this is most definitely, 100% certifiably, a dead duck."

The Vet turned to his computer terminal, hit a few keys and produced a bill, which he handed to the woman.

The duck's owner, still in shock, took the bill. "$150?" she cried, "$150 just to tell me my duck is dead!"

The Vet shrugged, "I'm sorry. If you had just taken my word for it, the bill would have been $20, but with the Lab Report and the CAT scan, it's now $150."

## Blind As A Bat

A vampire bat came flapping in from the night covered in fresh blood and parked himself on the roof of the cave to get some sleep.

Pretty soon all the other bats smelled the blood and began hassling him about where he got it.

He told them to knock it off and let him get some sleep but they persisted in hassling him to no end until finally he gave in.

"OK!" he said with exasperation, "Follow me," and he flew out of the cave with hundreds of bats following close behind him.

Down through the valley they went, across the river and into the deep forest. Finally he slowed down and all the other bats excitedly gathered around him.

"Do you see that tree over there?" he asked. "Yes, yes, yes!" the bats all screamed in a frenzy.

"Good," said the first bat, "Because I didn't!"

## Catholic Dog

Muldoon lived alone in the Irish countryside with only a pet dog for company.

One day the dog died, and Muldoon went to the parish priest and asked, "Father, my dog is dead. Could ya' be sayin' a Mass for the poor creature?"

Father Patrick replied, "I'm afraid not. We cannot have services for an animal in the church. But there are some Baptists down the lane, and there's no tellin' what they believe. Maybe they'll do something for the creature."

Muldoon said, "I'll go right away, Father. Do ya' think $5,000 is enough to donate to them for the service?"

Father Patrick exclaimed, "Sweet Mary, Mother of Jesus! Why didn't ya tell me the dog was Catholic?"

# Pest Control

A woman was having a passionate affair with an Irish inspector from a pest control company.

One afternoon they were carrying on in the bedroom together when her husband arrived home unexpectedly.

"Quick," said the woman to the lover, "Into the closet!" and she pushed him into the closet, stark naked.

The husband, however, became suspicious and after a search of the bedroom discovered the man in the closet.

"Who are you?" he asked him.

"I'm an inspector from Bugs-B-Gone," said the Exterminator.

"What are you doing in there?" the husband asked.

"I'm investigating a complaint about an infestation of moths," the man replied.

"And where are your clothes?" asked the husband.

The man looked down at himself and in a shocked voice said, "Those little bastards must have eaten them!"

# The Cow

Ole is a farmer in Minnesota. He needs a new milk cow, and hears about one for sale over in Nordakota. (That would be North Dakota for you non-Scandinavians.)

He drives to Nordakota, finds the farm and looks at the cow. He reaches under to see if she gives milk.

When he grabs the tit and pulls, the cow farts. Ole is surprised.

He reaches under the cow to try again.  He grabs another tit, pulls, and the cow farts again.  Milk does come out however, so after some discussion, Ole buys the cow and takes her home.

He gets back to Minnesota, and calls over his neighbor, Swede, and says, "Swede, come look at dis ere new cow I yust bought.  Pull her tit, and see vat happens."

So Swede reaches under, pulls the tit, and the cow farts.

Swede looks at Ole and says, "You bought dis here cow in Nordakota, din't yah?"

Ole is surprised since he hadn't told Swede about his trip and he replies, "Yah, dats right.  But how'd yah know?"

Swede says, "My wife's from Nordakota."

## The Lion Tamer

A circus owner runs an ad in a local newspaper- "Lion Tamer Wanted" and two people show up.

One is a retired golfer in his late-sixties and the other is a drop-dead, gorgeous brunette with a killer body in her mid-twenties.

The circus owner tells them, "I'm not going to sugar coat it.  This is one ferocious lion.  He ate my last tamer so you two had better be good or you're history."

"Here's your equipment-- a chair, a whip and a gun.  Who wants to try out first?"

The gorgeous brunette says, "I'll go first."  She walks past the chair, the whip and the gun and steps right into the lion's cage.

The lion starts to snarl and pant and begins to charge her.

As he gets close, the gorgeous brunette throws open her coat revealing her beautiful, perfect naked body.

The lion stops dead in his tracks, sheepishly crawls up to her and starts licking her feet and ankles. He continues to lick and kiss every inch of her body for several minutes, then lays down and rests his head at her feet.

The circus owner's jaw is on the floor!! He says, "That's amazing! I've never seen anything like that in my life!"

He then turns to the retired golfer and asks, "Can you top what you just saw in there?"

The tough old golfer replies, "Possibly, but you've got to get that lion out of there first."

## The Spider

I said to the wife, "Get me a newspaper."

"Don't be silly," she said. "Here, use my iPad."

That fuckin' spider never knew what hit it.

# Blondes

## Blond Guy

A Mexican, an Irishman and a blond guy were doing construction work on scaffolding on the 20th floor of a building.

They were eating lunch and the Irishman said, "Corned beef and cabbage! If I get corned beef and cabbage one more time for lunch, I'm going to jump off this building."

The Mexican opened his lunch box and exclaimed, "Burritos again! If I get burritos one more time I'm going to jump off, too."

The blond guy opened his lunch and said, "Bologna again! If I get a bologna sandwich one more time, I'm jumping too."

The next day, the Irishman opened his lunch box, saw corned beef and cabbage, and jumped to his death.

The Mexican opened his lunch, saw a burrito, and jumped, too.

The blond guy opened his lunch, saw the bologna and jumped to his death, as well.

At the funeral, the Irishman's wife was weeping.

She said, "If I'd known how really tired he was of corned beef and cabbage, I never would have given it to him again!"

The Mexican's wife also wept and said, "I could have given him tacos or enchiladas! I didn't realize he hated burritos so much."

Everyone turned and stared at the blond's wife. The blond's wife said, "Don't look at me. He makes his own lunch."

# Frozen Crabs

A lawyer boarded an airplane in New Orleans with a box of frozen crabs and asked a blonde flight attendant to take care of them for him. She took the box and promised to put it in the crew's refrigerator.

He advised her that he was holding her personally responsible for them staying frozen, mentioning, in an arrogant manner, that he was a lawyer, and threatened what would happen to her if she let them thaw out.

Shortly before landing in New York, she used the intercom to announce to the entire cabin, "Would the lawyer who gave me the crabs in New Orleans, please raise your hand?"

Not one hand went up. So, she took them home and ate them for dinner.

There are two lessons here:

1. Lawyers aren't as smart as they think they are.
2. Blondes aren't as dumb as most folks think.

# Irish Blonde

An attractive blonde from Cork, Ireland, arrived at the casino.

She seemed a little intoxicated and bet twenty thousand dollars on a single roll of the dice.

She said, "I hope you don't mind, but I feel much luckier when I'm completely nude."

With that she stripped from the neck down, rolled the dice and with an Irish brogue yelled, "Come on, baby, Mama needs new clothes!"

As the dicc came to a stop, she jumped up and down and squealed. "Yes! Yes! I won, I won!" She hugged each of the dealers, picked up her winnings and her clothes and quickly departed.

The dealers stared at each other dumbfounded.

Finally, one of them asked, "What did she roll?"

The other answered, "Damn if I know, I thought you were watching."

## Scuba Divers

A tourist asks a blond man, "Why do scuba divers always fall backwards off their boats?"

To which the blond man replies: "If they fell forward, they'd still be in the boat."

## Shampoo

A blond man is in the bathroom and his wife shouts, "Did you find the shampoo?"

He answers, "Yes, but I'm not sure what to do... it's for dry hair, and I've just wet mine."

## The Attempt

A blond man is in jail. The guard looks in his cell and sees him hanging by his feet.

"Just what are you doing?" he asks.

"Hanging myself," the blond replies.

"The rope should be around your neck" says the guard.

"I tried that," he replies, "but then I couldn't breathe."

# The Automobile

A blonde wanted to sell her car, but couldn't find any buyers.

She called her friend for advice, and her friend asked her how many miles she had on her car.

She said "235,000 miles."

Her friend told her that was the problem.

The blonde's friend told her that her brother is a mechanic and could roll back the miles to whatever she wanted.

So the blonde went to the mechanic and told him to set the miles at 40,000.

Two days later the blonde's friend asked her if she sold the car since her brother dropped the miles.

The blonde told her, "Why would I sell the car? There are only 40,000 miles on it!"

# The Blonde Policewoman

A blonde woman was speeding down the road with her little red sports car and was pulled over by a woman police officer, who also happened to be blonde.

The blonde cop asked to see the blonde driver's license. She dug through her purse and was getting progressively more agitated.

"What does it look like?" she finally asked.

The policewoman replied, "It's square and it has your picture on it."

The driver finally found a square mirror in her purse, looked at it, smiled with a sense of satisfaction and handed it over to the policewoman. "Here it is," she said.

The blonde officer looked at the mirror, then handed it back saying, "OK, you can go. I didn't realize that you were a cop."

## The Contractions

A blond man shouts frantically into the phone, "My wife is pregnant and her contractions are only two minutes apart!"

"Is this her first child?" asks the Doctor.

"No!" he shouts, "This is her husband!"

## The Goldfish

A blond man goes to the Vet with his goldfish.

"I think it's got epilepsy," he tells the Vet.

The Vet takes a look and says, "It seems calm enough to me."

The blond man says, "Wait, I haven't taken it out of the bowl yet."

## The Grenades

Two blond men find three hand grenades, and they decide to take them to a police station.

One asked, "What if one explodes before we get there?"

The other says: "We'll lie and say we only found two."

## The Missing Dog

A blond man's dog goes missing and he is frantic.

His wife says, "Why don't you put an ad in the paper?"

He does, but two weeks later the dog is still missing.

"What did you put in the paper?" his wife asks.

"Here boy!" he replies.

## The Truck Stop

A trucker came into a Truck Stop Cafe and placed his order.

He said, "I want three flat tires, a pair of headlights and a pair of running boards."

The brand new blonde waitress, not wanting to appear stupid, went to the kitchen and said to the cook, "This guy out there just ordered three flat tires, a pair of headlights and a pair of running boards. What does he think this place is, an auto parts store?"

"No," the cook said. "Three flat tires... mean three pancakes; a pair of headlights is two eggs sunny side up; and a pair of running boards is two slices of crisp bacon!"

"Oh... OK!" said the blonde.

She thought about it for a moment and then spooned up a bowl of beans and gave it to the customer.

The trucker asked, "What are the beans for, Blondie?"

She replied, "I thought while you were waiting for the flat tires, headlights and running boards, you might as well gas up!"

# Too Blonde To Know Better

On a plane bound for New York, the flight attendant approached a blonde woman sitting in the first class section and requested that she move to the economy section since she didn't have a first class ticket.

The blonde replied, "I'm blonde, I'm beautiful, I'm going to New York and I'm not moving."

Not wanting to argue with a customer, the flight attendant asked the co-pilot to speak to her.

He went to talk to the woman, asking her to please move out of the first class section.

Again, the blonde replied, "I'm blonde, I'm beautiful, I'm going to New York and I'm not moving."

The co-pilot returned to the cockpit and asked the captain what he should do. The captain replied, "I'm married to a blonde and I know how to handle this."

So, he went to the first class section and whispered in the blonde's ear.

She immediately jumped up and ran to the economy section, mumbling to herself, "Why didn't anyone just say so?"

Surprised, the flight attendant and the co-pilot asked the captain what he said to her.

The captain replied, "I told her the first class section wasn't going to New York."

# Drunks

## Crocked

Paddy had been drinking at his local Dublin pub all day and most of the night celebrating St. Patrick's Day.

At one point, Mick the bartender says, "You'll not be drinking anymore tonight, Paddy."

Paddy replies, "OK Mick, I'll be on my way then." Paddy spins around on his stool and steps off. He falls flat on his face.

"Damn," he says and pulls himself up by the stool and dusts himself off. He takes a step towards the door and falls flat on his face again.

"Damn, damn!"

He looks to the doorway and thinks to himself that if he can just get to the door and some fresh air, he'll be fine. He belly crawls to the door and shimmies up to the door frame. He sticks his head outside and takes a deep breath of fresh air, feels much better and takes a step out onto the sidewalk and falls flat on his face.

"By Jeebers… I'm a little crocked," he says.

He can see his house just a few doors down, and crawls to the door, hauls himself up the door frame, opens the door and shimmies inside.

He takes a look up the stairs and says, "No damn way." He crawls up the stairs to his bedroom door and says, "I can make it to the bed!" He takes a step into the room and falls flat on his face.

He says "Damn it!" He hauls himself up and falls into the bed.

The next morning, his wife, Jess, comes into the room carrying a cup of coffee and says, "Get up Paddy. Did you have a bit to drink last night?"

Paddy says, "No Jess, what makes you say that?"

"Mick phoned… you left your wheelchair at the pub."

## Even A Drunk Should Know Better

A drunk gets up from the bar and heads for the bathroom.

A few minutes later, a loud, blood-curdling scream is heard from the bathroom. Then, nothing.

After another minute or two, another loud scream reverberates through the bar.

The bartender goes into the bathroom to investigate why the drunk is screaming.

"What's all the screaming about in there?" he yells. "You're scaring my customers!"

"I'm just sitting here on the toilet minding my own business," says the drunk, "And every time I try to flush, something comes up and squeezes the hell out of my nuts."

The bartender opens the door, looks in, and says, "You idiot!"

"You're sitting on the mop bucket."

## Fishing

The rain was pouring down.

And there, standing in front of a big puddle outside the pub, was an old Irishman, drenched, and holding a stick with a piece of string dangling in the water.

A passerby stopped and asked, "What are you doing?"

"Fishing," replied the old man.

Feeling sorry for the old man, the gent says, "Come in out of the rain and have a drink with me."

In the warmth of the pub, as they sip their whiskey, the gentleman cannot resist asking, "So how many have you caught today?"

"You're the eighth," said the old man."

## The Costume Party

An older man walks into a bar wearing a stovepipe hat, a waistcoat and a phony beard.

He sits down at a bar and orders a drink.

As the bartender sets the drink down, he asks, "Going to a party?"

"Yeah, a costume party," the man answers, "I'm supposed to come dressed as my love life."

"But you look like Abe Lincoln," protests the bartender.

"That's right. My last four scores were seven years ago."

## The Worst Day

A drunk at a bar was just staring at his drink. He stays this way for half an hour.

Then, this big trouble-making truck driver steps next to him, takes the drink from the guy, and just drinks it all down. The poor man starts crying.

The truck driver says, "Come on man, I was just joking. Here, I'll buy you another drink. I just can't stand to see a man cry."

"No, it's not that. It's just that this day is the worst day of my life…"

"First, I fell asleep, and I get to my office late. My boss, outraged, fires me. When I leave the building, and head towards my car, I find out it was stolen."

"The police said that they can do nothing. I get a cab to return home, and when I leave the cab, I remember I left my wallet and credit cards there. The cab driver just drives away."

"I go home, and when I get there, I find my wife in bed with the gardener. I leave home, and come to this bar."

"And just when I was thinking about putting an end to my life, you show up and drink my cyanide and rat-poisoned beer."

# Ethnic

## Becoming An Irishman

Seven-year-old Mohammad entered his classroom on the first day of school.

"What's your name?" asked the teacher.

"Mohammad," he replied.

"You're in Ireland now," replied the teacher, "So from now on you will be known as Mike."

Mohammad returned home after school.

"How was your day, Mohammad?" his mother asked.

"My name is not Mohammad. I'm in Ireland and now my name is Mike."

"Are you ashamed of your name? Are you trying to dishonor your parents, your heritage and your religion? Shame on you!"

And his mother beat the shit out of him.

Then she called his father, who beat the shit out of him again.

The next day Mohammad returned to school. The teacher saw all of his fresh bruises.

"What happened to you, Mike?" she asked.

"Well shortly after becoming an Irishman, I was attacked by two fucking Muslims."

# An Irish Family Tradition

Paddy had long heard the stories of an amazing family tradition. It seems that his father, grandfather and great-grandfather had all been able to walk on water on their 18th birthdays.

On that special day, they'd each walked across the lake to the pub on the far side of the lake for their first legal drink.

So when Paddy's 18th birthday came around, he and his pal Mick took a boat out to the middle of the lake.

Paddy stepped out of the boat -- and nearly drowned! Mick just barely managed to pull him to safety.

Furious and confused, Paddy returned home and went to see his grandmother.

He asked her, "Grandma, 'tis me 18th birthday, so why can't I walk across the lake like me father, his father and his father before him?"

Granny looked deeply into Paddy's troubled blue eyes and said, "Because ye father, ye grandfather and ye great-grandfather were all born in December, when the lake is frozen, and ye were born in August, ya fookin' idiot!"

# Burning Eyes

Two black guys were in a bar talking, and one says to the other, "You ever notice that after you have sex with a white woman, your eyes burn, your nose burns and you get all teary-eyed?"

The second black guy says, "Yeah, all the time."

The first one asked, "Why is that?"

The second says, "I'm pretty sure it's the pepper spray."

# Luigi's Shoes

Luigi walks to work 20 blocks every day and passes a shoe store twice every day.

Each day he stops and looks in the window to admire a pair of Armani leather shoes. He wants those shoes so much...it's all he can think about.

After about two months, he saves the price of the shoes, $300, and purchases them.

Every Friday night, the Italian community holds a dance in the church basement.

Luigi seizes this opportunity to wear his new Armani leather shoes for the first time.

He asks Sophia to dance and as they dance he asks her, "Sophia, do you wear red panties tonight?"

Startled, Sophia replies, "Yes, Luigi, I do wear red panties tonight, but how do you know?"

Luigi answers, "I see the reflection in my new $300 Armani leather shoes. How do you like them?"

Next, he asks Rosa to dance, and after a few minutes he asks, "Rosa, do you wear white panties tonight?"

Rosa answers, "Yes, Luigi I do, but how do you know that?"

He replies, "I see the reflection in my new $300 Armani leather shoes. How do you like them?"

Now as the evening is almost over and the last song is being played, Luigi asks Carmela to dance.

Midway through the dance his face turns red.

He states, "Carmela, be stilla my heart. Please, please tell me you wear no panties tonight. Please, please, tella me this true!"

Carmela smiles coyly and answers, "Yes Luigi, I wear no panties tonight..."

Luigi gasps, "Thanka goodness. I thought I had a crack in my $300 Armani leather shoes!"

## Mexicans in a Row Boat

A U.S. Navy destroyer stops four Mexicans rowing a small boat towards Texas.

The Captain gets on the megaphone and shouts, "Ahoy, small craft. Where are you headed? "

One of the Mexicans puts down his oar, stands up, and shouts, "Gringo, we are invading the United States of America to reclaim the territory taken by the USA during the 1800s."

The entire crew on the destroyer doubles over in laughter. The Captain finally catches his breath, gets back on the megaphone and asks, "Just the four of you?"

The same Mexican stands up again and shouts, "No Senor, we are the last four. The other 21 million are already there."

## Get To Heaven

I was testing children in my Dublin Sunday school class to see if they understood the concept of getting to heaven.

I asked them, "If I sold my house and my car, had a big garage sale and gave all my money to the church, would that get me into heaven?"

"NO!" the children shouted.

"If I cleaned the church every day, mowed the garden, and kept everything tidy, would that get me into heaven?"

Again, the answer was "NO!"

"If I gave sweets to all the children and loved my husband, would that get me into heaven?"

Again, they all shouted, "NO!"

I was just bursting with pride for them. I continued, "Then how can I get into heaven?"

A little boy shouted out: "YUV GOTTA BE FOOKN' DEAD."

## Italian Grandfather

An old Italian man is dying. He calls his grandson to his bedside, "Guido, I wann'a you lissina me. I wann'a you to takea my chrome plated .38 revolver so you will always remember me."

"But Grandpa, I really don't like guns. How about you leave me your Rolex watch instead?"

"You lissina me, boy. Somma day you gonna be runna da business, you gonna have a beautiful wife, lotsa money, a big-a home and maybe a couple of bambinos."

"Somma day you gonna come-a home and maybe finda you wife inna bed with another man."

"Whatta you gonna do then? Pointa to you watch and say, 'times up?'"

## Last Wishes

Morris Schwartz is on his deathbed, knows the end is near, and is with his nurse, his wife, his daughter and two sons.

"So," he says to them, "Bernie, I want you to take the Beverly Hills houses."

"Sybil, take the apartments over in Los Angeles Plaza."

"Hymie, I want you to take the offices over in City Center."

"Sarah, my dear wife, please take all the residential buildings downtown."

The nurse is just blown away by all this and as Morris slips away, she says, "Mrs. Schwartz, your husband must have been such a hardworking man to have accumulated all this property."

Sarah replies, "Property??? The asshole has a paper route!"

## Poor MacDuffy

MacDuffy was walking home late at night and sees a woman in the shadows.

"Thirty euros," she whispers.

MacDuffy had never been with a hooker before but decides, what the hell, its only thirty euros.

So they hide in the bushes.

They're going 'at it' for a few minutes when all of a sudden a light flashes on them.

It is a policeman.

"What's going on here, people?" asks the policeman.

"I'm makin' love to me wife," Paddy answers sounding annoyed.

"Oh, I'm sorry," says the cop, "I didn't know."

"Well, neidder did I 'til ya shined that fooken light in her face!"

# Sex In The Shower

In a recent survey carried out for a leading toiletries firm, people from Chicago have proven to be the most likely to have had sex in the shower!

In the survey, 86% of Chicago's inner city residents say that they have enjoyed sex in the shower. The other 14% said they hadn't been to prison yet.

# The Comparison

What's the difference between an illegal Mexican and ET?

ET looked better, smelled better, learned English, didn't claim benefits, had his own fucking bike, and wanted to go home!

# The Countdown

Sorry for not calling you on New Year's, but I just got out of jail.

I was locked up for punching the shit out of this idiot at a party.

In my defense, when you hear an Arab counting down from 10, your instincts kick in.

# The Raffle

Some guy just knocked on my door selling raffle tickets for poor black orphans.

I said, "Fuck that! Knowing my luck, I'd win one!"

# The Prodigal Daughter

An Irishman's daughter had not been home for ten years.

Upon her return, her father yelled at her, "Where have ye been all this time? Why did ye not write to us? Not even a line. Why didn't ye call?"

"Can ye not understand what ye put yer old Mother thru?"

The girl, crying, replied, "Dad, I was too embarrassed. I became a prostitute."

"Ye what? Get out of here, ye shameless hussy! Sinner! You're a disgrace to this Catholic family, so ye are."

"OK, Daddy, as ye wish. I just came back to give Mammy this luxurious fur coat, a title deed to an eight bedroom mansion plus a $5 million check. For me little brother Seamus, this gold Rolex. And for ye Daddy, the sparkling new Mercedes limited edition convertible that's parked outside, plus a membership to the Limerick Country Club."

She takes a breath and continues, "And an invitation for ye all to spend New Year's Eve on board my new yacht in the Caribbean."

"Now what was it ye said ye had become?" asks Daddy.

The girl, crying again says, "A prostitute, Daddy!"

"Oh! Be Jesus! Ye scared me half to death, girl! I thought ye said a PROTESTANT. Come here and give yer old Daddy a big hug...... "

# The Towel

No matter what Isaac, the husband, did in bed, his wife never achieved an orgasm. Since, by Jewish law, a wife is entitled to sexual pleasure, they decide to consult their Rabbi.

The Rabbi listens to their story, strokes his beard, and makes the following suggestion:

"Hire a strapping young man.  While the two of you are making love, have the young man wave a towel over you.  That will help your wife fantasize and should bring on an orgasm."

They go home and follow the Rabbi's advice.

They hire a handsome young man and he waves a towel over them as they make love.

It does not help and the wife is still unsatisfied.

Perplexed, they go back to the Rabbi.

"Okay," he says to the husband, "This is a very special case, try it reversed.  Have the young man make love to your wife and you wave the towel over them."

Once again, they follow the Rabbi's advice.

They go home and hire the same strapping young man.

The young man gets into bed with the wife and the husband waves the towel, vigorously.

The young man gets to work with great enthusiasm and soon she has an enormous, room-shaking, ear-splitting, screaming orgasm.

The husband smiles, looks at the young man and says to him triumphantly, "See that, you schmuck?  THAT'S how you wave a towel!"

## The Wedding Night

A sweet and innocent young Italian girl gets married, but the girl's mother lives downstairs.

The girl has never made love to a man before, and on their wedding night, when he takes off his shirt, she goes running downstairs.

"Momma, Momma," she cries. "I can't believe it! He has hair all over his chest! What should I do?"

The mother is making spaghetti sauce.

She stirs the sauce thoughtfully and says, "Hair on his chest? He's your husband, it's your wedding night, go back upstairs."

When the girl gets back upstairs, the man takes off his pants. This sends her running back down to her mother.

"Momma, Momma! He has hair all over his legs! What should I do?"

The mother again stirs the sauce thoughtfully and says, "Hair on his legs? He's your husband, it's your wedding night, go back upstairs."

The girl goes back upstairs, and the man takes off his shoes and socks.

She looks down and sees that half of one of his feet is missing. She goes crying back down the stairs.

"Momma, Momma! He's got a foot and a half! What should I do?"

The mother hands her daughter the spoon and says, "A foot and a half?"

"Here, you stir the sauce. I'll go upstairs."

# Family

## A Day At The Beach

A mother and father take their 6-year old son to a family nude beach.

As the boy walks along the sand, he notices that many of the women have boobs bigger than his mother's, so he goes back to ask her why.

She tells her son, "The bigger they are, the sillier the lady is."

The boy, pleased with the answer, goes to play in the ocean but returns to tell his mother that many of the men have larger things than his dad does.

She replies, "The bigger they are, the dumber the man is."

Again satisfied with her answer, the boy goes back to the ocean to play.

Shortly thereafter, the boy returns and promptly tells his mother,

"Daddy is talking to the silliest lady on the beach, and the longer he talks, the dumber he gets."

## Farmer's Boy

A little boy comes down to breakfast. Since they live on a farm, his mother asks if he had done his chores.

"Not yet," said the little boy.

His mother tells him no breakfast until he does his chores.

Well, he's a little pissed off, so he goes to feed the chickens, and he kicks a chicken. He goes to feed the cows, and he kicks a cow. He then goes to feed the pigs, and he kicks a pig.

He goes back in for breakfast and his mother gives him a bowl of dry cereal.

"How come I don't get any eggs and bacon? Why don't I have any milk in my cereal?" he asks.

"Well," his mother says, "I saw you kick a chicken, so you don't get any eggs for a week. I saw you kick the pig, so you don't get any bacon for a week either. I saw you kick the cow so, for a week, you aren't getting any milk."

Just then, his father comes down for breakfast and kicks the cat halfway across the kitchen.

The little boy looks up at his mother with a smile and says, "You gonna tell him or should I?"


## Hello


Rrriiiiinnnnggg, rrriiiiinnnnggg,

"Hello?"

"Hi honey. This is Daddy. Is Mommy near the phone?"

"No, Daddy. She's upstairs in the bedroom with Uncle Gabe."

A brief pause….

Daddy says, "But honey, you haven't got an Uncle Gabe."

"Oh yes I do, and he's upstairs in the room with Mommy, right now."

Brief pause again….

"Uh, okay then, this is what I want you to do."

"Put the phone down on the table, run upstairs and knock on the bedroom door and shout to Mommy that Daddy's car just pulled into the driveway."

"Okay, Daddy, just a minute."

A few minutes later the little girl comes back to the phone. "I did it, Daddy."

"And what happened, honey?"

"Well, Mommy got all scared, jumped out of bed with no clothes on and ran around screaming."

"Then she tripped over the rug and hit her head on the dresser."

"And now she isn't moving at all!"

"Oh my God!!! What about your Uncle Gabe?"

"He jumped out of the bed with no clothes on, too."

"He was all scared and he jumped out of the back window and into the swimming pool."

"But I guess he didn't know that you took out the water last week to clean it."

"He hit the bottom of the pool and I think he's dead."

Long pause….

Longer pause….

Even longer pause….

Then Daddy says, "Swimming Pool………?"

"Is this 486-5731?"

"No, I think you have the wrong number."

# Little Girl

A little girl goes to the barbershop with her father.

She stands next to the barber's chair, eating a muffin, while her dad gets his haircut.

The barber smiles at her and says, "Sweetheart, you're gonna get hair on your muffin."

"I know," she replied, "And I'm gonna grow big tits too..."

# The Tinkle

A woman, pregnant with triplets, was walking down the street when a masked robber ran out of a bank and shot her three times in the stomach. Luckily the babies were alright and she recovered fully.

The surgeon decided to leave the bullets in because it was too risky to operate to remove them.

She gave birth to two healthy daughters and a healthy son.

All was fine for 16 years, and then one daughter walked into the room, in tears.

"What's wrong?" asked the mother.

"I was taking a tinkle and this bullet came out," replied the daughter.

The mother told her it was okay and explained what had happened 16 years ago.

About a week later, the second daughter walked into the room, in tears.

"Mom, I was taking a tinkle and this bullet came out."

Again the mother told her not to worry and explained what had happened 16 years earlier.

A week later her son walked into the room, in tears.

"It's okay," said the Mom, "I know what happened. You were taking a tinkle and a bullet came out."

"No," said the boy, "I was playing with myself and I shot the dog."

## Robot

A father buys a lie-detector robot that slaps people when they lie.

He decides to test it out at dinner one night.

The father asks his son what he did that afternoon.

The son says, "I did some school work." The robot slaps the son.

The son says, "OK, OK! I was at a friend's house watching movies."

Dad asks, "What movie did you watch?"

Son says, "Toy Story." The robot slaps the son.

Son says, "OK, OK! We were watching porn."

Dad says, "What? At your age I didn't even know what porn was." The robot slaps the father.

Mom laughs and says, "Well, he certainly is your son!" The robot slaps the mother.

ROBOT FOR SALE.

## The Proposition

An elderly grandfather, his son and grandson went to the country club for their weekly round of golf.

Just as they reached the first tee, a beautiful young blonde woman carrying her bag of clubs approached them.  She explained that the member who brought her to the club for a round of golf had an emergency that called him away and asked the trio whether she could join them.

Naturally, the guys all agreed.

Smiling, the blonde thanked them and said, "Look, fellas, I work in a topless bar as a dancer, so nothing shocks me anymore.  If any of you want to smoke cigars, have a beer, bet, swear, tell off-color stories or do anything that you normally do when playing a round together, go ahead.  But, I enjoy playing golf, and consider myself pretty good at it, so don't try to coach me on how to play my shots."

With that, the guys agreed to relax and invited her to drive first.  All eyes were fastened on her shapely behind as she bent to place her ball on the tee.  She then took her driver and hit the ball 270 yards down the middle-right of the fairway in front of the green.

The father's mouth was agape.  "That was beautiful," he said.

The blonde put her driver away and said, "I really didn't get into it, and I faded it a little."

After the three guys hit their drives and their second shots, the blonde took out an eight iron and lofted the ball within five feet of the hole.

The son said, "Damn, lady, you played that perfectly."

The blonde frowned and said, "It was a little weak, but even an easy seven would have been too much club.  I've left a tricky little putt."

She then tapped in the five-footer for a birdie.

Having the honors, she drove first on the second hole, knocked the heck out of the ball, and it landed nearly 300 yards away smack in the middle of the fairway.

For the rest of the round, the statuesque blonde continued to amaze the guys, quietly and methodically shooting for par or less on every hole.

When they arrived at the 18th green, the blonde was three under par, and had a very nasty 12- foot putt on an undulating green for a par.

She turned to the three guys and said, "I really want to thank you all for not acting like a bunch of chauvinists and telling me what club to use or how to play a shot, but I need this putt for a 69 and I'd really like to break 70 on this course."

"If any one of you can tell me how to make par on this hole, I'll take him back to my apartment, pour some 35-year-old Single Malt Scotch in him, fix him a steak dinner and then show him a very good time the rest of the night."

The yuppie grandson jumped at the thought!  He strolled across the green, carefully eyeing the line of the putt and finally said, "Honey, aim about 6 inches to the right of the hole and hit it firm.  It will get over that little hump and break right into the cup."

The father knelt down and sighted the putt using his putter as a plumb. "Don't listen to the kid, darlin', you want to hit it softly 10 inches to the right and let it run left down that little hogback, so it falls into the cup."

The old gray-haired grandfather walked over to the blonde's ball, picked it up and handed it to her and said, "That's a gimme, sweetheart."

The blonde smiled and said, "Your car or mine?"

## Three Sons

A father told his three sons, when he sent them to the University, "I feel it is my duty to provide you with the best education possible, and you do not owe me anything for providing that.  However, I want you to honor my last wish."

"As a token, I want each of you to put $1,000 into my coffin when I die."

And so it happened.

His sons became a doctor, a lawyer, and a financial planner, each very successful financially.

When their father's time had come and they saw their father in the coffin, they remembered his wish.

First, it was the doctor who put 10- $100 bills onto the chest of the deceased.

Then, came the financial planner, who also put $1,000 there.

Finally, it was the heartbroken lawyer's turn.

He reached into his jacket pocket, took out his checkbook, wrote a check for $3,000, put it into his father's coffin, and took the $2,000 cash.

He later went on to become a member of Congress...

# Friends

## Good Ole Boys

Joe died in a fire and his body was burned pretty badly. The morgue needed someone to identify the body, so they sent for his two best deer hunting friends, Cooter and Guber.

The three men had always hunted and fished together and were long time members of a hunt camp.

Cooter arrived first, and when the mortician pulled back the sheet, Cooter said, "Yup, his face is burned up pretty bad."

"You better roll him over." The mortician rolled him over and Cooter said, "Nope, ain't Joe."

The mortician thought this was rather strange, so he brought Guber in to confirm the identity of the body.

Guber looked at the body and said, "Yup, he's pretty well burnt up. Roll him over."

The mortician rolled him over and Guber said, "No, it ain't Joe."

The mortician asked, "How can you tell?"

Guber said, "Well, Joe had two assholes."

"What! He had two assholes?" asked the mortician.

"Yup, we never seen 'em, but everybody used to say, 'There's Joe with them two assholes.'"

# Reunions

A group of 15-year-old boys discussed where to meet for dinner.

It was agreed they'd meet at McDonalds next to Captain Jacks Seafood Grille because they only had 6 dollars among them, they could ride their bikes there, and Jennie Webster [the cute girl in Social Studies] lives on the same street, and they might see her.

Ten years later, the group of now 25 year old guys discussed where they should meet for dinner. It was agreed they would meet at Captain Jack's Seafood Grille because the beer was cheap, the bar had free snacks, the house band was good, there was no cover charge and there were lot of cute girls.

Ten years later, at 35 years of age, the group once again discussed where they should meet for dinner. It was decided they would meet at Captain Jack's Seafood Grille because the booze was good, it was near their gym and, if they went late enough, there wouldn't be too many whiny little kids.

Ten years later, at 45, the group once again discussed where they should meet for dinner. It was agreed they would meet at Captain Jack's Seafood Grille because the martinis were big and the waitresses wore tight pants.

Ten years later, now 55, the group once again discussed where they should meet for dinner. It was agreed they would meet at Captain Jack's Seafood Grille because the prices were reasonable, they have a nice wine list and fish is good for your cholesterol.

Ten years later, at 65 years of age, they once again group discussed where they should meet for dinner. It was agreed they would meet at Captain Jack's Seafood Grille because the lighting was good and they have an early bird special.

Ten years later, at 75 years of age, the group once again discussed where they should meet for dinner. It was agreed they would meet at Captain Jack's Seafood Grille because the food was not too spicy and the restaurant was handicapped accessible.

Ten years later, at 85 years of age, the group once again discussed where they should meet for dinner.  It was agreed they would meet at Captain Jack's Seafood Grille because they had never been there before.

## The River

Three men were hiking through a forest when they came upon a raging and violent river.

Needing to get to the other side, the first man prayed, "God, please give me the strength to cross the river."

Poof!  God gave him big arms and strong legs…... and he was able to swim across in about 2 hours, having almost drowned twice.

After witnessing that, the second man prayed, "God, please give me strength and the tools to cross the river."

Poof!  God gave him a boat and strong arms and strong legs…... and he was able to row across in about an hour, after almost capsizing once.

Seeing what happened to the first two men, the third man prayed, "God, please give me the strength, the tools and the intelligence to cross the river."

Poof!  HE WAS TURNED INTO A WOMAN!

She checked the map, hiked one hundred yards upstream...... and walked across the bridge.

## Four Ladies

Four lady friends meet at their thirtieth-year school reunion.  One goes to the bar to get some drinks while the other three start to talk.

The first lady says her son studied economics, became a banker and is so rich, he gave his best friend a Ferrari.

The second said her son became a pilot, started his own airline, became so rich, he gave his best friend a jet.

The third said her son became an engineer, started his own development company, became so rich, he built his best friend a mansion.

When the fourth friend came back with a plate full of food, she asked what the buzz was about and they told her that all three had very successful sons and asked about her son.

She paused and then told them that her son is gay and he works in a Gay Bar.

After a pause one of the friends asked softly if she was disappointed …. ?

"Oh noooo!!" said the lady, "He is doing well.  Last week, on his birthday, he got a Ferrari, a jet and a mansion from three of his boyfriends."

All three ladies fainted….

## Three Women Golfers

Three women are playing the 4th hole at Crow Canyon Golf course when a naked man, wearing a bag over his head, jumps from the trees and runs across the green.

The three women look and are in shock at the size of his manhood.

The first woman says, "Well he definitely is not my husband."

The second woman looks at his manhood and says, "He, for sure, is not my husband."

The third woman takes a good look and says "He's not even a member of this club."

# Little Ralphy

## Little Ralphy On Getting Older

Little Ralphy was sitting on a park bench munching on one candy bar after another.

After the 6th one, a man on the bench across from him said, "Son, you know eating all that candy isn't good for you. It will give you acne, rot your teeth, and make you fat."

Little Ralphy replied, "My grandfather lived to be 107 years old."

The man asked, "Did your grandfather eat 6 candy bars at a time?"

Little Ralphy answered, "No, he minded his own fucking business."

## Little Ralphy On Math

A teacher asks her class, "If there are 5 birds sitting on a fence and you shoot one of them, how many will be left?"

She calls on Little Ralphy.

He replies, "None, they will all fly away with the first gunshot."

The teacher replies, "The correct answer is 4, but I like your thinking."

Then Little Ralphy says, "I have a question for YOU."

"There are 3 women sitting on a bench having ice cream. One is delicately licking the sides of the triple scoop of ice cream. The second is gobbling down the top and sucking the cone. The third is biting off the top of the ice cream."

"Which one is married?"

The teacher, blushing a great deal, replied, "Well, I suppose the one that's gobbled down the top and sucked the cone."

To which Little Ralphy replied, "The correct answer is the one with the wedding ring on, but I like your thinking."


## Little Ralphy On Math Again

Little Ralphy returns from school and says he got an F in arithmetic.

"Why?" asks the father.

"The teacher asked "How much is 2 times 3 and I said 6," replies Ralphy.

"But that's right!" says his dad.

"Yeah, but then she asked me 'How much is 3 times 2?"

"What's the fucking difference?" asks the father.

Little Ralphy replied, "That's what I said!"


## Little Ralphy On Vocabulary

Little Ralphy goes to school, and the teacher says, "Today we are going to learn multi-syllable words, class. Does anybody have an example of a multi-syllable word?"

Ralphy says "Mas-tur-bate."

Miss Rogers smiles and says, "Wow, little Ralphy, that's a mouthful."

Little Ralphy says, "No, Miss Rogers, you're thinking of a blowjob."

# Little Ralphy On Writing

One day, during lessons on Proper Grammar, the teacher asked for a show of hands from those who could use the word "beautiful" in the same sentence twice.

First, she called on little Suzie, who responded with, "My father bought my mother a beautiful dress and she looked beautiful in it."

"Very good, Suzie," replied the teacher. She then called on little Michael.

"My mummy planned a beautiful banquet and it turned out beautifully."

She said, "Excellent, Michael!" Then the teacher reluctantly called on Little Ralphy.

Little Ralphy said, "Last night at the dinner table, my sister told my father that she was pregnant and he said, "Beautiful, just fucking beautiful!"

# The Polite Way to Pee

During one of her daily classes, a teacher, trying to teach good manners, asked her students the following question:

"Michael, if you were on a date having dinner with a nice young lady, how would you tell her you have to go to the bathroom?"

Michael said, "Excuse me, I need to pee."

The teacher responded, "That would be quite impolite. What about you Sherman, how would you say it?"

Sherman said, "I am sorry, but I really need to go to the bathroom. I'll be right back."

"That's better, but it's still not very nice to say the word 'bathroom' at the dinner table.  And you, Ralphy, can you use your brain for once and show us your good manners?"

Little Ralphy said, "I would say 'Darling, may I please be excused for a moment?  I have to shake hands with a very dear friend of mine, whom I hope to introduce to you after dinner.'"

# Marriage

## Boys Night Out

The missus asked me, "When you're on a boys' only trip, do you think about me?"

Apparently, "Only to stop myself from cumming too quickly" wasn't the right answer.

## Mad Cow

I took my wife to a restaurant. The waiter, for some reason, took my order first.

"I'll have the rump steak, rare, please."

He said, "Aren't you worried about the mad cow?"

"Nah, she can order for herself."

## Marriage Certificate

Wife: "What are you doing?"

Husband: "Nothing."

Wife: "Nothing? You've been reading our marriage certificate for an hour."

Husband: "I was looking for the expiry date."

## Courtesy

Son: "Mom, when I was on the bus with Dad this morning, he told me to give up my seat to a lady."

Mom: "Well, you have done the right thing."

Son: "But Mom, I was sitting on Daddy's lap."

## Dinner Is Served

A man comes home from a hard day of work only to find his wife laying in front of the fireplace, stark naked, with her legs spread wide open.

He asked, "Honey, what are you doing?"

She replied, "I'm heating up your dinner."

## Dust

My wife sat down next to me as I was flipping channels.

She asked, "What's on TV?"

I said, "Lots of dust."

## Fortune

A newly married man asked his wife, "Would you have married me if my father hadn't left me a fortune?"

"Honey," the woman replied sweetly, "I'd have married you, no matter who left you a fortune!"

# Missing Person

A husband went to the sheriff's department to report that his wife was missing.

Husband: "My wife is missing. She went shopping yesterday and has not come home."

Sergeant: "What is her height?"

Husband: "Gee, I'm not sure. A little over five-feet tall."

Sergeant: "Weight?"

Husband: "Don't know. Not slim, not really fat."

Sergeant: "Color of eyes?"

Husband: "Sort of brown, I think. Never really noticed."

Sergeant: "Color of hair?"

Husband: "Changes a couple times a year. Maybe dark brown now. I can't remember."

Sergeant: "What was she wearing?"

Husband: "Could have been pants, or maybe a skirt or shorts. I don't know exactly."

Sergeant: "What kind of car did she drive?"

Husband: "She went in my truck."

Sergeant: "What kind of truck was it?"

Husband: "A 2015 Ford F150 King Ranch 4X4 with eco-boost 5.0L V8 engine, special ordered with manual transmission and climate controlled air conditioning. It has a custom matching white cover for the bed, which has a matching aftermarket bed liner, custom leather 6-way seats and

"Bubba" floor mats, a trailering package with a gold hitch and special wiring hook-ups, a DVD with full GPS navigation, satellite radio receiver, 23-channel CB radio, six cup holders, a USB port, and four power outlets. I added special alloy wheels and off-road Michelins. It has custom running boards and indirect wheel-well lighting."

At this point, the husband started to choke up.

Sergeant: "Don't worry, buddy. We'll find your truck."

## Girls Night Out

Two women friends had gone out for a "Girls Night Out," and had been decidedly over-enthusiastic on the cocktails. Incredibly drunk and walking home, they suddenly realized they both needed to pee.

They were very near a graveyard and one of them suggested they do their business behind a headstone or something.

The first woman had nothing to wipe with so she took off her panties, used them and threw them away.

Her friend, however, was wearing an expensive underwear set and didn't want to ruin hers, but was lucky enough to salvage a large ribbon from a wreath that was on a grave and proceeded to wipe herself with it.

After finishing, they made their way home.

The next day the first woman's husband phones the other husband and said, "These damn girls' nights out have got to stop. My wife came home last night without her panties."

"That's nothing," said the other. "Mine came back with a ribbon and sympathy card stuck between the cheeks of her butt that said, 'From all of us at the Fire Station. We'll never forget you!'"

# Golf Buddies

After a round of golf, a guy brings his best golf mate home, unannounced, for dinner at 6:30 pm.

His wife screams her head off while his friend sits open mouthed and listens to the tirade.

"My bloody hair and makeup are not done, the house is a fucking mess and the dishes aren't done.  Can't you see I'm still in my fucking pajamas and I can't be bothered with cooking tonight!  Why the fuck did you bring him home, unannounced, you stupid idiot?"

"Because he's thinking of getting married."

# Husbands

A man was sitting, reading his paper, when his wife hit him on the head with a frying pan.

"What was that for?" the man asked.

The wife replied, "That was for the piece of paper with the name "Betty" on it that I found in your trouser pocket."

The man then said, "When I was at the races last week, Betty was the name of the horse I bet on."

The wife apologized and went on with the housework.

Three days later the man is watching TV when his wife bashes him on the head with an even bigger frying pan, knocking him unconscious.

Upon regaining consciousness, the man asked why she had hit him again.

Wife replied, "Your horse phoned!"

# In A Hurry

My wife just came in and said, "I don't know if I am coming or going."

I said to her, "Judging by the look on your face, you're going, 'cus when you're coming, you look like a fucking Down Syndrome kid trying to whistle!"

# Infidelity

An old man asks his wife, "Martha, soon we will be married 50 years, and there's something I have to know. In all of these 50 years, have you ever been unfaithful to me?"

Martha replied, "Well Henry, I have to be honest with you. Yes, I've been unfaithful to you three times during these 50 years, but always for a good reason."

Henry was obviously hurt by his wife's confession, but said, "I never suspected. Can you tell me what you mean by 'good reasons'?"

Martha said, "The first time was shortly after we were married, and we were about to lose our little house because we couldn't pay the mortgage."

"Do you remember that one evening I went to see the banker and the next day he notified you that the loan would be extended?"

Henry recalled the visit to the banker and said, "I can forgive you for that. You saved our home, but what about the second time?"

Martha asked, "And do you remember when you were so sick, but we didn't have the money to pay for the heart surgery you needed? Well, I went to see your doctor one night and, if you recall, he performed the surgery at no charge."

"I recall that," said Henry, "And you did it to save my life, so of course I can forgive you for that.  Now tell me about the third time."

"Alright," Martha said.  "Do you remember when you ran for president of your golf club, and you needed 73 more votes?"

Henry fainted...

## Reincarnation

A wife was talking to her husband about reincarnation.

"What exactly is reincarnation?" he asked.

"It's when you die and come back as something completely different," she explained.

"So," he suggested, "I could come back as a pig?"

She sighed wearily. "You're not listening, are you?"

## Social Security

After retiring, I went to the Social Security office to apply for benefits.

The woman behind the counter asked me for my driver's license to verify my age.

I looked in my pockets and realized I had left it at home.  I told the woman I would have to go home and come back later.

The woman said, "Unbutton your shirt."

So I opened my shirt revealing my curly silver chest hair.

She said, "That silver hair on your chest is proof enough for me" and she processed my Social Security application.

When I got home, I told my wife about my experience at the Social Security office.

She said, "You should have dropped your pants. You might have gotten disability too."

## The Beers

A guy gets a call from the police telling him that his house was robbed.

The offenders had also consumed all of his beer and had raped his wife.

A moment of silence passes, then the guy says, "I can't believe they screwed my wife after only five beers!"

## The Breakup

He spent the first day following his divorce packing his belongings into boxes, crates and suitcases. On the second day, he had the movers come and collect his things.

On the third day, he sat down for the last time at their beautiful dining room table by candlelight, put on some soft background music, and feasted on a pound of shrimp, a jar of caviar, and a bottle of spring water.

When he had finished, he went into each and every room and deposited a few half-eaten shrimp shells, dipped in caviar, into the hollow ends of the curtain rods. He then cleaned up the kitchen and left.

When his ex-wife returned with her new partner, all was bliss for the first few days.

Then slowly, the house began to smell. They tried everything- cleaning, mopping and airing the place out. Vents were checked for dead rodents, and carpets were steam cleaned. Air fresheners were hung everywhere.

Exterminators were brought in to set off gas canisters, during which time they had to move out for a few days, and in the end, they even paid to replace the expensive wool carpeting.

Nothing worked!!

People stopped coming over to visit. Repairmen refused to work in the house. The maid quit. Finally, they could not take the stench any longer and decided to move.

A month later, even though they had cut their price in half, they could not find a buyer for their stinky house. Word got out and eventually even the local realtors refused to return their calls. Finally, they had to borrow a huge sum of money from the bank to purchase a new place.

The ex-husband called and asked her how things were going. She told him the saga of the rotting house. He listened politely and said that he missed his old home terribly and asked if she would be willing to reduce her divorce settlement in exchange for getting the house.

Knowing he had no idea how bad the smell was, they agreed on a price that was about 1/10th of what the house had been worth, but only if he were to sign the papers that very day. He agreed and within the hour his lawyers delivered the paperwork.

A week later the ex and her partner stood smiling as they watched the moving company pack everything to take to their new home.

And just to spite her ex-husband, they even took the curtain rods!

## The Earring

A man is at work one day when he notices that his co-worker is wearing an earring.

The man knows his co-worker to be a normally conservative fellow, and is curious about his sudden change in "fashion sense."

The man walks up to him and says, "I didn't know you were into earrings."

"It is not such a big deal, it's only an earring," he replies sheepishly.

His friend falls silent for a few minutes, but then his curiosity prods him to ask, "So, how long have you been wearing one?"

"Ever since my wife found it in my car."

## The Escaped Convict

A man escapes from prison where he has been for 15 years.

He breaks into a house to look for money and guns and finds a young couple in bed.

He orders the guy out of bed and ties him to a chair while tying the girl to the bed. He gets on top of her, kisses her neck, then gets up and goes into the bathroom.

While he's in there, the husband tells his wife, "Listen, this guy's an escaped convict, look at his clothes!"

"He's probably spent lots of time in jail and hasn't seen a woman in years. I saw how he kissed your neck. If he wants to sleep with you, don't resist, don't complain, do whatever he tells you. Satisfy him no matter how much he nauseates you. This guy is probably very dangerous. If he gets angry, he'll kill us. Be strong, honey. I love you."

To which his wife responds, "He wasn't kissing my neck. He was whispering in my ear. He told me he was gay, thought you were cute, and asked me if we had any Vaseline."

"I told him it was in the bathroom. Be strong honey. I love you too!"

## The Fart

This is a story about a couple who had been married for many years.

The only friction in their marriage was the husband's habit of farting very loudly every morning when he awoke. The noise would wake his wife and the smell would make her eyes water and make her gasp for air.

Every morning she would plead with him to stop ripping them off because it was making her sick. He told her he couldn't stop it and that it was perfectly natural. She told him to see a doctor because she was concerned that one day he would blow his guts out.

The years went by and he continued to rip them out.

Then one Christmas Day morning, as she was preparing the turkey for dinner, she looked at the innards, neck, gizzard, liver and all the other spare parts of the turkey and a malicious thought came to her.

As he was sound asleep, she took the bowl of turkey parts and went upstairs to their bedroom. She gently pulled the bed covers back, pulled the elastic waistband of his underpants and emptied the bowl of turkey guts into his shorts.

Sometime later, she heard her husband awaken with his usual trumpeting which was followed by a blood-curdling scream and the sound of frantic footsteps as he ran into the bathroom.

The wife could hardly control herself as she rolled on the floor laughing, with tears in her eyes.

After years of torture, she reckoned she got him back pretty good.

About twenty minutes later, her husband came downstairs in his bloodstained underpants with a look of horror on his face. She bit her lip as she asked what the matter was.

He said, "Honey, you were right. All these years you have warned me and I didn't listen to you."

"What do you mean?" asked his wife.

"Well, you always told me that one day I would end up farting my guts out, and today it finally happened. But.... by the grace of God.... and with some Vaseline and two fingers, I think I got most of them back in."

# The Final Answer

My wife and I were watching "Who Wants To Be A Millionaire" while we were in bed.

I turned to her and said, "Do you want to have sex?"

"No," she answered.

I then said, "Is that your final answer?"

She didn't even look at me this time, simply saying, "Yes."

So I said, "Then I'd like to phone a friend."

# The Genie

A husband takes his wife to play her first round of golf.

Of course, the wife promptly hacked her first shot right through the window of the biggest house adjacent to the course.

The husband cringed, "I warned you to be careful! Now we'll have to go up there, find the owner, apologize and see how much your lousy drive is going to cost us."

So the couple walked up to the house and knocked on the door.

A warm voice said, "Come on in."

When they opened the door they saw the damage that was done. Glass was all over the place, and a broken antique bottle was lying on its side near the pieces of window glass.

A man reclining on the couch asked, "Are you the people who broke my window?"

"Uh...yeah, sir. We're sure sorry about that," the husband replied.

"Oh, no apology is necessary. Actually, I want to thank you. I'm a Genie, and I've been trapped in that bottle for a thousand years. Now that you've released me, I'm allowed to grant three wishes. I'll give you each one wish, but if you don't mind, I'll keep the last one for myself."

"Wow, that's great!" the husband said. He pondered a moment and blurted out, "I'd like a million dollars a year for the rest of my life."

"No problem," said the Genie. "You've got it, it's the least I can do. And I'll guarantee you a long and healthy life!"

"And now you, young lady, what do you want?" the Genie asked.

"I'd like to own a gorgeous home in every country in the world complete with servants," she said.

"Consider it done," the Genie said. "And your homes will always be safe from fire, burglary and natural disasters!" "And now," the couple asked in unison, "What's your wish, Genie?"

"Well, since I've been trapped in that bottle, and haven't been with a woman in more than a thousand years, my wish is to have sex with your wife."

The husband looked at his wife and said, "Gee, honey, you know we both now have a fortune, and all those houses. What do you think?"

She mulled it over for a few moments and said, "You know, you're right. Considering our good fortune, I guess I wouldn't mind, but what about you, honey?"

"You know I love you sweetheart," said the husband. "I'd do the same for you!"

So the Genie and the woman went upstairs where they spent the rest of the afternoon enjoying each other. The Genie was insatiable.

After about three hours of non-stop sex, the Genie rolled over and looked directly into her eyes and asked, "How old are you and your husband?"

"Why, we're both 35," she responded breathlessly.

"No kidding," he said. "Thirty-five years old and you both still believe in Genies?"

## The Lawn Mower

When our lawn mower broke, my wife kept nagging me to get it fixed. But, I always had something else to take care of.

Finally she thought of a clever way to make her point.

I found her seated in the tall, unmowed grass, busily snipping away with a tiny pair of scissors.

I watched silently for a short time and then went into the house. I was gone only a minute, and when I came out again I handed her a toothbrush.

I said, "When you finish cutting the grass, you might as well sweep the driveway."

The doctors say I will walk again, but I will always have a limp.

## The Measurement

Got this text from my brother-in-law recently.

It read: "Can I stay at your house for a while? The ol' lady kicked me out after she caught me measuring my dick. For what it's worth, it reaches all the way to the back of her sister's throat!"

## The New Perfume

I bought a new perfume for my wife called "Chloroform," but she says she doesn't like it.

She says that it makes her sleepy and her ass sore.

# The Reunion

My wife was at her high school reunion, and she kept staring at a drunk swigging his drink as he sat alone at a nearby table.

I asked her, "Do you know him?"

"Yes", she sighed, he's my old boyfriend. He began drinking right after we split up years ago, and hasn't been sober since."

"My God!" I said, "Who would think a person could go on celebrating that long?"

# The Shopping Trip

A husband and wife are shopping in their local store.

The husband picks up a case of Budweiser and puts it in the cart.

"What do you think you're doing?" asks the wife.

"They're on sale, only $10 for 24 cans," he says. "Put 'em back, we can't afford them," demands the wife.

They continue shopping.

A few aisles farther on, the woman picks up a $20 jar of face cream and puts it in the basket.

"What do you think you're doing?" asks the husband.

"It's my face cream. It makes me look beautiful," the wife says.

Her husband retorts, "So does 24 cans of Budweiser and it's half the price!"

# Vern's Funeral

Vern works hard at the Phone Company but spends two nights each week bowling, and plays golf every Saturday.

His wife thinks he's pushing himself too hard, so for his birthday, she takes him to a local Strip Club.

The doorman at the club greets them and says, "Hey, Vern! How ya doin?"

His wife is puzzled and asks if he's been to this club before.

"Oh no," says Vern. "He's in my bowling league."

When they are seated, a waitress asks Vern if he'd like his usual and brings over a Budweiser.

His wife is becoming increasingly uncomfortable and says, "How did she know that you drink Budweiser?"

"I recognize her, she's the waitress from the golf club. I always have a Bud at the end of the 1st nine, honey."

A stripper then comes over to their table, throws her arms around Vern, starts to rub herself all over him and says..."Hi Vern. Want your usual table dance, big boy?"

Vern's wife, now furious, grabs her purse and storms out of the club.

Vern follows and spots her getting into a cab. Before she can slam the door, he jumps in beside her.

Vern tries desperately to explain how the stripper must have mistaken him for someone else. But his wife is having none of it.

She is screaming at him at the top of her lungs, calling him every four letter word in the book.

The cabby turns around and says, "Geez Vern, you picked up a real bitch this time."

VERN'S FUNERAL WILL BE HELD THIS COMING FRIDAY.

# Medical

## Dentist Visit

A man goes to a female dentist to have a tooth extracted. She pulled out a large syringe to give an anesthesia shot.

"No way, no needles! I hate needles!" the man exclaimed.

So she started to hook up the nitrous oxide tank, and the man said, "I can't do the gas thing. Just the thought of having a mask on my face suffocates me!"

The dentist then asked the patient if he had any objections to taking a pill. "No," he says, "I'm fine with pills."

So the dentist gave him two little blue pills and he swallowed them.

"What are those?" he asked.

"Viagra," she replied.

"I'll be damned," said the patient, "I didn't know Viagra worked as a pain killer."

"It doesn't," said the dentist, "But it will give you something to hold on to when I pull your tooth."

## Doctors At A Funeral

A very prestigious cardiologist died, and was given a very elaborate funeral by the hospital he worked for most of his life.

A huge heart, covered in flowers stood behind his casket during the services.

All the doctors from the hospital sat in awe.

Following the eulogy, the heart opened and the casket rolled inside.

The heart closed, sealing the doctor inside of the beautiful heart forever.

At that point, one of the mourners just burst into laughter.

With all eyes staring at him, he said, "I'm sorry, I was just thinking of my own funeral… I'm a gynecologist."

The proctologist fainted.

## Farts

A little old lady goes to the doctor.

He asks her, "What seems to be the problem?"

She says, "Doctor, I have this problem with gas, but it really doesn't bother me too much. My farts never smell, and are always silent. As a matter of fact, I've farted at least 20 times since I've been here in your office. You didn't know I was farting because they don't smell and are silent."

The doctor says, "I see, take these pills and come back to see me next week."

The next week, the lady returns for her follow-up appointment.

"Doctor," she says, "I don't know what you gave me, but now my farts, although still silent, stink terribly."

The doctor says, "Good! Now that we've cleared up your sinuses, let's work on your hearing."

## The Dentist

A guy and a girl meet at a bar. They get along so well that they decide to go to the girl's place.

A few drinks later, the guy takes off his shirt and then washes his hands. He then takes off his trousers and again washes his hands.

The girl has been watching him and says, "You must be a dentist."

The guy, surprised, says, "Yes .... How did you figure that out?"

"Easy..." she replies, "you keep washing your hands."

One thing leads to another and they make love.

After it's over the girl says, "You must be a good dentist."

The guy, now with an inflated ego, says, "Sure, I'm a good dentist. How did you figure that out?"

The girl replies, "Didn't feel a thing."

## The Doctor's Office

I went to the doctor's office the other day and found out that my new doctor is young, female and drop dead gorgeous.

I was embarrassed, but she said, "Don't worry, I'm a professional. I've seen it all before. Just tell me what's wrong and I'll check it out."

I said, "My wife thinks that my dick tastes funny."

## The Gynecologist

A beautiful woman went to the gynecologist. The doctor took one look at the woman and all his professionalism flew out the window. He immediately told her to get undressed.

After she disrobed, the doctor began to stroke her thigh.

While doing so he asked her, "Do you know what I am doing?"

"Yes," she replied, "You are checking for abrasions or dermatological abnormalities."

"That's right," said the doctor. He then began to fondle her breasts.

"Do you know what I am doing now?" he asked.

"Yes," she said, "You are checking for lumps which might indicate breast cancer."

"Correct," replied the shady doctor.

Finally, he mounted his patient and started having sexual intercourse with her.

He asked, "Do you know what I am doing now?"

"Yes," she said, "You're getting syphilis. That's why I came here in the first place."

## The Medical Convention

A doctor addressed his audience:

"The material we put into our stomachs should have killed most of us sitting here, years ago. Red meat is full of steroids and dye. Soft drinks corrode your stomach lining. Chinese food is loaded with MSG. High transfat diets can be disastrous and none of us realize the long-term harm caused by germs in our drinking water. But, there is one thing that is the most dangerous of all and most of us have had, or will eat it."

"Can anyone tell me what food it is that causes the most grief and suffering for years after eating it?"

After several seconds of quiet, a 70-year-old man in the front row raised his hand, and softly said, "Wedding Cake."

# The Pharmacist

A nice, calm and respectable lady went into the pharmacy, walked up to the pharmacist, looked straight into his eyes, and said, "I would like to buy some cyanide."

The pharmacist asked, "Why in the world do you need cyanide?"

The lady replied, "I need it to poison my husband."

The pharmacist's eyes grew big and he exclaimed, "Lord have mercy! I can't give you cyanide to kill your husband. That's against the law! I'll lose my license! They'll throw both of us in jail! All kinds of bad things will happen. Absolutely not! You CANNOT have any cyanide!"

The lady reached into her purse and pulled out a picture of her husband in bed with the pharmacist's wife.

The pharmacist looked at the picture and replied, "Well now, that's different. You didn't tell me you had a prescription."

# The Tonsils

"You'll be fine," the doctor said after finishing the young woman's surgery.

"But," she asked, "How long will it be before I am able to have a normal sex life again doctor?"

The surgeon seemed to pause and his face reddened as a small tear ran down his cheek from the corner of his eye. The girl was alarmed.

"What's the matter Doctor? I will be all right, won't I?"

He replied, "Yes, you'll be fine. It's just that no one has ever asked me that after having tonsils removed."

# What's In A Name

A psychiatrist was conducting a group therapy session with four young mothers and their small children.

"You ALL have obsessions," he observed.

To the first mother, Mary, he said, "You are obsessed with eating. You've even named your daughter, Candy."

He turned to the second Mom, Ann, and said, "Your obsession is with money.  Again, it manifests itself in your child's name, Penny."

He turned to the third Mom, Joyce, and said, "Your obsession is alcohol. This too shows itself in your child's name, Brandy."

At this point, the fourth mother, Kathy, quietly got up, took her little boy by the hand, and whispered, "Come on, Dick, this guy has no idea what he's talking about.   I'm running late and need to pick up Peter and Willie from school."

# Politics

## Eternal Life

A guy is walking along a Florida beach when he comes across a lamp partially buried in the sand.

He picks up the lamp and gives it a rub.

A genie appears and tells him he has been granted one wish.

The guy thinks for a moment and says, "I want to live forever."

"Sorry," said the genie, "I'm not allowed to grant eternal life."

"OK, then. I want to die after the Democrats balance the budget and eliminate the national debt."

"You crafty little bastard," said the genie.

## Pay Your Bills

Once upon a time there lived a beautiful Queen with incredible large breasts.

Nick, the Dragon Slayer, was obsessed over the Queen for this reason. He knew that the penalty for his desire would be death should he try to touch them, but he had to try.

One day, Nick revealed his secret desire to his colleague, Horatio, the Physician, the King's chief doctor.

Horatio thought about this and said that he could arrange for Nick to more than satisfy his desire, but it would cost him 1000 gold coins to arrange it. Without pause, Nick readily agreed to the scheme.

The next day, Horatio made a batch of itching powder and poured a little bit into the Queen's bra while she bathed. Soon after she dressed, the itching commenced and grew intense.

Upon being summoned to the Royal Chambers to address this incident, Horatio informed the King and Queen that only a special saliva, if applied for four hours, would cure this type of itch. Tests have shown that, among all of the citizens of the kingdom, only the saliva of Nick would work as the antidote to cure the itch.

The King, eager to help his Queen, quickly summoned Nick to their chambers.

Horatio then slipped Nick the antidote for the itching powder, which he put into his mouth, and for the next four hours, Nick worked passionately on the Queen's large and magnificent breasts.

The Queen's itching was eventually relieved, and Nick left satisfied and was hailed by both the King and Queen as a hero.

Upon returning to his chamber, Nick found Horatio demanding his payment of 1000 gold coins.

With his obsession now satisfied, Nick couldn't have cared less knowing that Horatio could never report this matter to the King and, with a laugh, told him to get lost.

The next day, Horatio slipped a massive dose of the same itching powder into the King's underwear.

The King immediately summoned Nick.

## President's Day

I was eating breakfast with my 10-year-old granddaughter and I asked her, "What day is tomorrow?"

Without skipping a beat she said, "It's Presidents Day!"

69

She's smart, so I asked her, "What does Presidents Day mean?"

I was waiting for something about Trump, Obama, Bush, or Clinton.

She replied, "Presidents Day is when the President steps out of the White House, and if he sees his shadow, we have another year of Bullshit."

You know, it hurts when hot coffee spurts out your nose.

# Relationships

## A Man And A Woman in Bed

A man and a woman were fast asleep in bed. Suddenly, at 4 o'clock in the morning, a resounding noise came from outside.

The woman, sort of bewildered, jumps up from the bed and yells at the man, "Oh no! That must be my husband!"

The man quickly got out of bed, panicked and naked. He jumped out the window like a crazy man, smashed on the ground, picked himself up and went straight through a thorn bush. Then he stood up and started to run as fast as he could to his car.

A few minutes later the door opens and the man is standing at it, panting hard, with dirt and scratches all over him. He yells, "I'm your husband, you idiot!"

And the woman answers: "Oh, yeah? And why were you running, you bastard?"

## The Barbershop

A guy stuck his head into a barbershop and asked, "How long before I can get a haircut?"

The barber looked around the shop full of customers and said, "About 2 hours."

The guy left.

A few days later, the same guy stuck his head in the door and asked, "How long before I can get a haircut?"

The barber looked around at the shop and said, "About 3 hours."

The guy left.

A week later, the same guy stuck his head in the shop and asked, "How long before I can get a haircut?"

The barber looked around the shop and said, "About an hour and a half."

The guy left.

The barber turned to his friend and said, "Hey, Bob, do me a favor, follow him and see where he goes."

"He keeps asking how long he has to wait for a haircut, but he never comes back."

A little while later, Bob returned to the shop, laughing hysterically.

The barber asked, "So, where does he go when he leaves?"

Bob looked up, wiped the tears from his eyes and said, "Your house."

## Being A Farmer

A farmer was selling his peaches door to door.

He knocked on a door and a shapely 30-something woman dressed in a very sheer negligee answered the door.

He raised his basket to show her the peaches and asked, "Would you like to buy some peaches?"

She pulled the top of the negligee to one side and asked, "Are they as firm as this?"

He nodded his head and said, "Yes ma'am," and a little tear ran from his eye.

Then she pulled the other side of her negligee off asking, "Are they nice and pink like this?"

The farmer said, "Yes," and another tear came from the other eye.

Then she unbuttoned the bottom of her negligee and asked, "Are they as fuzzy as this?"

He again said, "Yes," and broke down crying.

She asked, "Why on earth are you crying?"

Drying his eyes he replied, "The drought got my corn, the flood got my soy beans, a tornado leveled my barn, and now I think I'm going to get fucked out of my peaches."

## Computer Dating

A young lady visited a computer dating service and requested, "I'm looking for a spouse. Can you please help me find a suitable one?"

The matchmaker said, "What exactly are you looking for?"

"Well, let me see. He needs to be good looking, polite, humorous, sporty and knowledgeable. He must be willing to accompany me the whole day at home, if I don't go out, be amazing in bed when I need a companion and be silent when I want to rest."

The matchmaker entered the information into the computer and, in a matter of moments, handed the results to the woman.

The results read, "BUY A DILDO."

## Heaven

A woman wanted to know how she could get into Heaven.

God told her to give up smoking, drinking and sex if she wants to get into

Heaven. The woman said she would try her best.

God visited the woman a week later to see how she was getting on.

"Not bad," said the woman. "I've given up smoking and drinking, but then I bent over to look in the refrigerator freezer and when my boyfriend caught sight of my long slender legs, he pulled up my skirt, pulled my panties to one side and made love to me right then and there."

"They don't like that in Heaven," God said.

The woman replied, "They're not too happy about it in Costco either!"

## Sensitive Man

A woman meets a man in a bar. They talk, they connect, and they end up leaving together.

They go back to his place, and as he shows her around his apartment, she notices that one wall of his bedroom is completely filled with soft, sweet, cuddly teddy bears.

There are three shelves in the bedroom, with hundreds and hundreds of cute, cuddly teddy bears carefully placed in rows, covering the entire wall.

It was obvious that he had taken quite some time to lovingly arrange them. She was immediately touched by the amount of thought he had put into organizing the display.

There were small bears all along the bottom shelf, medium-sized bears covering the length of the middle shelf, and huge, enormous bears running all the way along the top shelf.

She found it strange for an obviously masculine guy to have such a large collection of Teddy Bears.

She is quite impressed by his sensitive side, but doesn't mention this to him.

They share a bottle of wine, continue talking and, after a while, she finds herself thinking, "Oh my God!  Maybe, this guy could be the one! Maybe he could be the future father of my children?"

She turns to him and kisses him lightly on the lips.  He responds warmly.

They continue to kiss, the passion builds and he romantically lifts her in his arms and carries her into his bedroom, where they rip off each other's clothes and make hot, steamy love.

She is so overwhelmed that she responds with more passion, more creativity and more heat than she has ever known.

After an intense, explosive night of raw passion with this sensitive guy, they are lying there together in the afterglow.

The woman rolls over, gently strokes his chest and asks coyly, "Well, how was it?"

The guy gently smiles at her, strokes her cheek, looks deeply into her eyes and says,

"Help yourself to any prize from the middle shelf."

## Sleeping Arrangements

A man and a woman who had never met before and both married to other people, found themselves assigned to the same sleeping room on a transcontinental train.

Though initially embarrassed and uneasy over sharing a room, they were both very tired and fell asleep quickly- him in the upper bunk and she in the lower.

At 1:00 AM, the man leaned over and gently woke the woman saying, "Ma'am, I'm sorry to bother you, but would you be willing to reach into the closet to get me a second blanket? I'm awfully cold."

"I have a better idea," she replied.  "Just for tonight, let's just pretend that we're married."

"Wow! That's a great idea!" he exclaimed!

"Good," she replied... "GET YOUR OWN FUCKING BLANKET!!!"

After a stunned moment of silence, he farted.

## The Accident

I rear-ended a car this morning . . . the start of a really bad day!

The driver got out of the other car, and I noticed that he was a DWARF!!

He looked up at me and said, "I am NOT happy!"

So I said, "Well, which one ARE you then?"

## The Ammo

One morning, an old Mississippi farm hand was able to buy two boxes of ammo.

He placed the boxes on the front seat of his car and headed back home, but stopped at a gas station where a drop-dead gorgeous blonde, in a short skirt, was filling up her car at the next pump.

She glanced at the two boxes of ammo, bent over and leaned in his passenger window, and said in a sexy voice, "I'm a big believer in barter, old fella. Would you be interested in trading sex for ammo?"

He thought for a few seconds, then asked, "Sure 'nuff, what kind of ammo ya got?"

## The Back Door

I was banging this nice lady on her kitchen table when we heard the front door open.

She said, "It's my husband!  Quick, try the back door!"

Thinking back, I really should have ran, but you don't get offers like that every day.

## The Boots

A teacher was helping one of her pupils put on his boots.

He asked for help and she could see why.

Even with her pulling, and him pushing, the little boots still didn't want to go on.  By the time they got the second boot on, she had worked up a sweat.

She almost cried when the little boy said, "Teacher, they're on the wrong feet."  She looked, and sure enough, they were.

Unfortunately, it wasn't any easier pulling the boots off, than it was putting them on.

She managed to keep her cool as, together, they worked to get the boots back on, this time on the correct feet.

He then announced, "These aren't my boots."  She bit her tongue, rather than get right in his face and scream.

She smiled at the little boy, but did not say a word.

Once again, she struggled to help him pull the ill-fitting boots off his little feet.

No sooner had they got the boots off when he said, "They're my brother's boots.  But my Mom made me wear 'em today."

Now she didn't know if she should laugh or cry.

But she mustered up what grace and courage she had left to wrestle the boots back onto his feet again.

Helping him into his coat, she asked, "Now, where are your mittens?"

He said, "I stuffed 'em in the toes of my boots.  I didn't want to lose them!!!!"

# The Elevator

Today, I was beaten up by this gorgeous young woman.

I was in the elevator on the fifth floor this morning, minding my own business, when this lovely girl entered.

As I was staring at her boobs, she said to me, "Would you please press One...?"

So I did...........

# The Factory

There is a factory in Essex which makes the Tickle Me Elmo toys.  The toy laughs when you tickle it under the arms.

Well, Shelley is hired at The Tickle Me Elmo factory and she reports for her first day promptly at 8:00 am.

The next day at 8:45 am there is a knock at the Personnel Manager's door.  The Foreman throws open the door and begins to rant about the new employee.

He complains that she is incredibly slow and the whole line is backing up, putting the entire production line behind schedule.

The Personnel Manager decides he should see this for himself, so the two men march down to the factory floor.  When they get there, the line is so backed up that there are Tickle Me Elmo's all over the factory floor and they're really beginning to pile up.  At the end of the line stands Shelley surrounded by mountains of Tickle Me Elmo toys.

She has a roll of plush red fabric and a huge bag of small marbles.

The two men watch in amazement as she cuts a little piece of fabric, wraps it around two marbles and begins to carefully sew the little package between Elmo's legs.

The Personnel Manager bursts into laughter. After several minutes of hysterics, he pulls himself together and approaches Shelley.

"I'm sorry," he says to her, barely able to keep a straight face, "but I think you misunderstood the instructions I gave you yesterday."

"Your job is to give Elmo two test tickles."

## The Fortune Teller

I saw a fortune teller the other day. She told me I would come into some money.

Last night, I screwed a girl called Penny.

Is that spooky or what?

## The Gift

One year, I decided to buy my mother-in-law a cemetery plot as a Christmas gift.

The next year, I didn't buy her a gift.

When she asked me why, I replied,

"Well, you still haven't used the gift I bought you last year!"

## The Paratrooper

A young woman joined the Army and signed up with the paratroopers. She went through the standard training, completed the practice jumps from higher and higher structures, and finally went to take her first jump from an airplane.

The next day, she called home to tell her mother the news.

"So, did you jump?" asked the mother.

"Well, let me tell you what happened," the girl said. "We got up in the plane, and the sergeant opened up the door and asked for volunteers. About a dozen people got up and just walked to the door of the plane."

"Is that when you jumped?" asked her mother.

"Uh, no. The sergeant started to grab the other men, one at a time, and throw them out the door."

"Did you jump then?" asked her mother.

"I'm getting to that. Everyone else had jumped, and I was the last one left on the plane. I told the sergeant that I was too scared to jump. He told me to get off the plane or he'd kick my butt."

"So, did you jump?'

"No. He tried to push me out of the plane, but I grabbed onto the door and refused to go. Finally he called over the Jump Master. The Jump Master is this great big guy, about six-foot six, and 280 pounds. He said to me, 'Are you gonna jump or not?'"

I said, "No Sir, I'm too scared."

"So the Jump Master pulled down his zipper and took out his penis. I swear Mom, it was about ten inches long and as big around as a baseball bat! He said, 'Either you jump out that door, or I'm sticking this bad boy right up your ass.'"

"So, did you jump?" asked her mother.

"Well, a little at first."

# Religion

## Celibacy

A priest and a rabbi were sitting in adjacent seats on an airplane.

After a while the priest turned to the rabbi and asked, "Is it still a requirement of your faith that you not eat pork?"

The rabbi responded, "Yes, that is still one of our laws."

The priest then asked, "Have you ever eaten pork?"

"Yes, on one occasion I did succumb to temptation and ate a bacon sandwich."

The priest nodded in understanding and went on with his reading.

A while later the rabbi spoke up and asked, "Father, is it still a requirement of your church that you remain celibate?"

The priest replied, "Yes, that is still very much a part of our faith."

The rabbi then asked him, "Father, have you ever fallen to the temptations of the flesh?"

The priest replied, "Yes, Rabbi, on one occasion I was weak and broke the pledge of my faith."

The rabbi nodded understandingly and remained silent for several minutes.

Finally the rabbi quietly observed, "Beats the shit out of a bacon sandwich, doesn't it?"

# Donation

Father O'Malley answers the phone.

"Hello, is this Father O'Malley?"

"It is!"

"This is the Taxation Department. Can you help us?"

"I'll try!"

"Do you know a Ted Houlihan?"

"I do!"

"Is he a member of your congregation?"

"He is!"

"Did he donate $10,000 to the church?"

"He will!"

# Pearly Gates

A priest dies and is waiting in line at the Pearly Gates.

Ahead of him is a guy who's dressed in sunglasses, a loud shirt, leather jacket, and jeans.

Saint Peter addresses this cool guy, "Who are you, so that I may know whether or not to admit you to the Kingdom of Heaven?"

The guy replies, "I'm Bruce, retired airline pilot from Toronto."

Saint Peter consults his list. He smiles and says to the pilot, "Take this silken robe and golden staff and enter the Kingdom." The pilot then enters Heaven with his robe and staff.

Next, it's the priest's turn. He stands erect and booms out, "I am Father John, pastor of Saint Mary's for the last 43 years."

Saint Peter consults his list. He says to the priest, "Take this cotton robe and wooden staff and enter the Kingdom."

"Just a minute," says the good Father. "That man was a pilot and he gets a silken robe and golden staff and I get only cotton and wood. How can this be?"

"Up here - we go by results," says Saint Peter.

"When you preached, people slept. When he flew, people prayed."


## The Hospital Bill


A man suffered a serious heart attack while shopping in a store. The store clerk called 911 when he saw him collapse to the floor.

The paramedics rushed the man to the nearest hospital where he had emergency open heart surgery.
.
He awakened from the surgery to find himself in the care of nuns at the Catholic Hospital.

A nun was seated next to his bed holding a clipboard loaded with several forms, and a pen. She asked him how he was going to pay for his treatment.

"Do you have health insurance?" she asked.

He replied in a raspy voice, "No health insurance."

The nun asked, "Do you have money in the bank?"

He replied, "No money in the bank."

"Do you have a relative who could help you with the payments?" asked the irritated nun.

He said, "I only have a spinster sister, and she is a nun."

The nun became agitated and announced loudly, "Nuns are not spinsters! Nuns are married to God."

The patient replied, "Perfect. Send the bill to my brother-in-law."

## The New Church

A newlywed couple wanted to join a church.

The pastor told them, "We have special requirements for new parishioners. You must abstain from sex for an entire month."

The couple agreed and, after two and a half weeks, returned to the church.

When the Pastor ushered them into his office, the wife was crying, and the husband, obviously, was very depressed.

"You are back so soon. Is there a problem?" the pastor inquired.

"We are terribly ashamed to admit that we did not manage to abstain from sex for the required month," the young man replied sadly.

The pastor asked him what happened.

"Well, the first week was difficult. However, we managed to abstain through sheer will power. The second week was terrible, but with the use of prayer, we managed to abstain. The third week, however, was unbearable."

"We tried cold showers, prayer, reading from the Bible, anything to keep our minds free of carnal thoughts."

"But one afternoon, my wife reached for a can of paint and dropped it."

"When she bent over to pick it up, I noticed that she didn't have panties on and I was overcome with lust and I had my way with her, right then and there," admitted the man, shamefaced.

"You understand this means you will not be welcome into our church," stated the pastor.

"We know," said the young man, hanging his head.

"We're not welcome at Home Depot anymore, either."

## The Pay Raise

A pastor's wife was expecting a baby, so he stood before the congregation and asked for a raise in pay.

After much discussion, the congregation passed a rule that whenever the pastor's family expanded, so would his paycheck.

After 6 children, this started to get expensive and the congregation decided to hold another meeting to discuss the pastor's expanding salary.

A great deal of yelling and inner bickering ensued, as to how much the pastor's additional children were costing the church, and how much more it could potentially cost.

After listening to them for about an hour, the pastor rose from his chair and spoke, "Children are a gift from God, and we will take as many gifts as He gives us."

Silence fell over the congregation.

In the back pew, a little old lady struggled to stand, and finally said in her frail voice, "Rain is also a gift from God, but when we get too much of it, we wear rubbers."

The entire congregation said, "Amen."

# Seniors

## The Artist

An elderly woman decided to have her portrait painted.

She told the artist, "Paint me with diamond earrings, a diamond necklace, emerald bracelets, a ruby broach and a gold Rolex."

The confused artist said, "But you're not wearing any of those things."

"I know," she said. "But if I die before my husband, I'm sure my husband will remarry, and I want his new wife to go crazy looking for the jewelry."

## An Aging Cinderella

Cinderella is now 95 years old. After a fulfilling life with the now dead prince, she happily sits upon her rocking chair, watching the world go by from her front porch, with a cat named Bob for companionship.

One sunny afternoon, out of nowhere, appeared her fairy godmother.

Cinderella said, "Fairy Godmother, what are you doing here after all these years?"

The fairy godmother replied, "Cinderella, you have lived an exemplary life since I last saw you. Is there anything for which your heart still yearns?"

Cinderella was taken back, overjoyed, and after some thoughtful consideration, she uttered her first wish. "The prince was wonderful, but not much of an investor. I'm living hand to mouth on my disability checks, and I wish I were wealthy beyond comprehension."

Instantly her rocking chair turned into solid gold.

Cinderella said, "Oooh, thank you, Fairy Godmother."

The fairy godmother replied, "It is the least that I can do. What do you want for your second wish?"

Cinderella looked down at her frail body, and said, "I wish I was young and full of the beauty and youth that I once had." At once, her wish became reality, and her beautiful young body returned.

Cinderella felt stirrings inside of her that had been dormant for years.

And then the fairy godmother spoke once more. "You have one more wish, what shall it be?"

Cinderella looks over to the frightened cat in the corner and says,

"I wish for you to transform Bob, my old cat, into a kind and handsome young man."

Magically, Bob suddenly underwent so fundamental a change in his biological makeup, that when he stood before her, he was a man so beautiful, the likes of him neither she, nor the world, had ever seen.

The fairy godmother said, "Congratulations, Cinderella, enjoy your new life." And with a blazing shock of bright blue electricity, the fairy godmother was gone, as suddenly as she appeared.

For a few eerie moments, Bob and Cinderella looked into each other's eyes.

Cinderella sat, breathless, gazing at the most beautiful, stunning perfect man, she had ever seen.

Then Bob walked over to Cinderella, who was transfixed in her rocking chair, and held her close in his young muscular arms.

He leaned in close, blowing her golden hair with his warm breath, as he whispered….

"Bet you're sorry that you had me neutered."

# Brothel Trip

An elderly man goes into a brothel and tells the madam he would like a young girl for the night.

Surprised, she looks at the ancient man and asks how old he is.

"I'm 90 years old," he proudly says.

"90?" replies the woman, "Don't you realize that I think you've had it?"

"Oh, sorry," says the old man. "How much do I owe you?"

# Marriage Is Sharing

The old man placed an order for one hamburger, French fries and a drink.

He unwrapped the plain hamburger and carefully cut it in half, placing one half in front of his wife. He then carefully counted out the French fries, dividing them into two piles and neatly placed one pile in front of his wife. He took a sip of the drink, his wife took a sip and then set the cup down between them.

As he began to eat his few bites of hamburger, the people around them were looking over and whispering.

Obviously they were thinking, "That poor old couple - all they can afford is one meal for the two of them."

As the man began to eat his fries, a young man came to the table and politely offered to buy another meal for the old couple. The old man said that they were just fine - they were used to sharing everything. People closer to the table noticed the little old lady hadn't eaten a bite. She sat there watching her husband eat and occasionally taking turns sipping the drink.

Again, the young man came over and begged them to let him buy another meal for them. This time the old woman said, "No, thank you, we are used to sharing everything."

Finally, as the old man finished and was wiping his face neatly with the napkin, the young man again came over to the little old lady who had yet to eat a single bite of food and asked, "What is it you are waiting for?"

She answered, "THE TEETH."

## Confession

An elderly man walks into a confessional. The following conversation ensues:

Man: "I am 92 years old, and have a wonderful wife of 70 years, many children, grandchildren, and great grandchildren. Yesterday, I picked up two hitch-hiking college girls. We went to a motel where I had sex with each of them three times."

Priest: "Are you sorry for your sins?"

Man: "What sins?"

Priest: "What kind of a Catholic are you?"

Man: "Catholic? I'm Jewish."

Priest: "Why are you telling me all this?"

Man: "I'm 92 years old. . . I'm telling everybody!"

## Memories Of Grandma

My grandmother died in the 80's but her birthday is coming up, and that always causes me to reminisce.

The long walks we used to take to the shop in town, the 5 cents she gave me for meaningless jobs like pulling weeds or cleaning off the driveway. Her soothing hands when I would get hurt.

But the thing I remember most was her sage advice.

Once when I was about 13, we were sitting in the park enjoying a cookie and a Coke. She told me that one day I would find a wonderful woman and start my own family.

"Always remember this," she said. "Be sure you marry a woman with small hands."

"How come, Grandma?"

She smiled and said gently, "Makes your dick look bigger."

Grandma was special to me.

## Elderly Golfer

An elderly golfer comes in after a round of golf at the new course and heads straight to the bar/restaurant area of the club house. As he passes through the swinging doors, he spots a sign hanging over the bar that reads:

COLD BEER: $5.00
HAMBURGER: $10.00
CHEESEBURGER: $15.50
CHICKEN SANDWICH: $18.50
HAND JOB: $250.00

Checking his wallet to be sure he has the necessary money, the old golfer walks up to the bar and beckons to the exceptionally attractive female bartender, who is serving drinks to a couple of sun-wrinkled golfers.

She glides down behind the bar to the old golfer. "Yes?" she inquires with a wide, knowing smile. "May I help you, sir?"

The old golfer leans over the bar and whispers, "I was wondering young lady, are you the one who gives the hand jobs around here?"

She looks into his wrinkled eyes and with a wide smile purrs, "Yes sir, I sure am."

The old golfer leans in even closer and into her left ear says softly, "Well then, be sure to wash your hands real good, because I want a cheeseburger."

## Grandma's Birth Control Pills

After working most of her life, Grandma finally retired.

At her next checkup, her new doctor told her to bring a list of all the medicines that had been prescribed for her.

As the young doctor was looking through these, his eyes grew wide when he discovered she had a prescription for birth control pills.

"Mrs. Smith, do you realize these are BIRTH CONTROL pills?"

"Yes, they help me sleep at night."

"Mrs. Smith, I assure you there is absolutely NOTHING in these pills that could possibly help you sleep!"

She reached out and patted the young Doctor's knee.

"Yes, dear, I know that. But every morning, I grind one up and mix it in the glass of orange juice that my 16 year old granddaughter drinks...and believe me, it really helps me sleep at night."

## Peanuts

A tour bus driver is driving with a bus load of seniors down a highway when he is tapped on his shoulder by a little old lady.

She offers him a handful of peanuts, which he gratefully munches up.

After about 15 minutes, she taps him on his shoulder again and she hands him another handful of peanuts. She repeats this gesture about five more times.

When she is about to hand him another batch again, he asks the little old lady, "Why don't you eat the peanuts yourself?"

"We can't chew them because we've got no teeth," she replied.

The puzzled driver asks, "Why do you buy them then?"

The old lady replied, "We just love the chocolate around them."

## Rye Bread

Two old Jewish guys, one 80 and one 87, were sitting on a park bench one morning.

The 87-year-old had just finished his morning jog and wasn't even short of breath.

The 80-year-old was amazed at the guy's stamina and asked him what he did to have so much energy.

The 87-year-old said, "Well, I eat rye bread every day."

"It keeps your energy level high and you'll have great stamina with the ladies."

So, on the way home the 80-year-old stopped at the bakery.

As he was looking around, the saleslady asked if he needed any help.

He said, "Do you have any rye bread?"

She said, "Yes, there's a whole shelf of it. Would you like some?"

He said, "I want five loaves."

She said, "My goodness, five loaves!  By the time you get to the third loaf, it'll be hard."

He replied, "I can't believe everybody knows about this shit but me."

## The Obituary

A Scottish woman goes to the local newspaper office to see that the obituary for her recently deceased husband is published.

The obit editor informs her that there is a charge of 50 cents per word.

She pauses, reflects and then she says, "Well then, let it read, 'Angus Mac Pherson died.'"

Amused at the woman's thrift, the editor tells her that there is a seven word minimum for all obituaries.

She thinks it over and in a few seconds says, "In that case, let it read…………… 'Angus Mac Pherson died.  Golf clubs for sale.'"

# Points of View

## A Cajun's View On Terrorists

A City Councilman from Evangeline, Louisiana, was asked on a local live radio talk show, just what he thought about the allegations of torture of suspected terrorists.

His reply prompted his ejection from the studio, but to thunderous applause from the audience.

HIS STATEMENT: "If hooking up one raghead terrorist prisoner's testicles to a car battery to get the truth out of the lying little camelshagger will save just one Coonass's life, then I have only three things to say: "Red is positive, Black is negative, and make sure his nuts are wet.""

## 18 Reasons Why Fishing Is Better Than Sex

1- You don't have to hide your fishing magazines.
2- It is perfectly acceptable to pay a professional to fish with you once in a while.
3- The Ten Commandments don't say anything about fishing.
4- If your partner takes pictures or videotapes of you fishing, you don't have to worry about them showing up on the Internet if you become famous.
5- Your fishing partner doesn't get upset about people you fished with long ago.
6- It's perfectly respectable to fish with a total stranger.
7- When you see a really good fisherman, you don't have to feel guilty about imagining the two of you fishing together.
8- If your regular fishing partner isn't available, he/she won't object if you fish with someone else.
9- Nobody will ever tell you that you will go blind if you fish by yourself.
10- When dealing with a fishing pro, you never have to wonder if he is really an undercover cop.

11- You don't have to go to a sleazy shop in a seedy neighborhood to buy fishing stuff.

12- You can have a fishing calendar on your wall at the office, tell fishing jokes, and invite coworkers to fish with you without getting sued for harassment.

13- There are no fishing-transmitted diseases.

14- If you want to watch fishing on television, you don't have to subscribe to the Playboy channel.

15- Nobody expects you to fish with the same partner for the rest of your life.

16- Nobody expects you to give up fishing if your partner loses interest in it.

17- You don't have to be a newlywed to plan a vacation primarily to enjoy your favorite activity.

18- Your fishing partner will never say, "Not again?  We just fished last week!  Is fishing all you ever think about?"

## Complete and Finished

No English dictionary has been able to adequately explain the difference between these two words: "Complete" and "Finished."

In a recently held linguistic competition held in London and attended by supposedly the best in the world, a Guyanese man, was the clear winner with a standing ovation which lasted over 5 minutes.

The final question was: How do you explain the difference between COMPLETE and FINISHED in a way that is easy to understand?   Some people say there is NO difference between COMPLETE and FINISHED.

Here is his astute answer:

"When you marry the right woman, you are COMPLETE.  When you marry the wrong woman, you are FINISHED.  And when the right one catches you with the wrong one, you are COMPLETELY FINISHED!!"

# Hell Freezes Over

The following is an actual question given on a University of Arizona chemistry midterm, and an actual answer turned in by a student.

The answer by one student was so profound that the professor shared it with colleagues, via the Internet, which is, of course, why we now have the pleasure of enjoying it as well:  Bonus Question:  Is Hell exothermic (gives off heat) or endothermic (absorbs heat)?

Most of the students wrote proofs of their beliefs using Boyle's Law (gas cools when it expands and heats when it is compressed) or some variant.

One student, however, wrote the following:

"First, we need to know how the mass of Hell is changing in time.  So we need to know the rate at which souls are moving into Hell and the rate at which they are leaving, which is unlikely.  I think that we can safely assume that once a soul gets to Hell, it will not leave.  Therefore, no souls are leaving.  As for how many souls are entering Hell, let's look at the different religions that exist in the world today.

Most of these religions state that if you are not a member of their religion, you will go to Hell.  Since there is more than one of these religions and since people do not belong to more than one religion, we can project that all souls go to Hell.  With birth and death rates as they are, we can expect the number of souls in Hell to increase exponentially.  Now, we look at the rate of change of the volume in Hell because Boyle's Law states that in order for the temperature and pressure in Hell to stay the same, the volume of Hell has to expand proportionately as souls are added.

This gives two possibilities:

1. If Hell is expanding at a slower rate than the rate at which souls enter Hell, then the temperature and pressure in Hell will increase until all Hell breaks loose.

2. If Hell is expanding at a rate faster than the increase of souls in Hell, then the temperature and pressure will drop until Hell freezes over.

So which is it?

If we accept the postulate given to me by Teresa during my Freshman year that, 'It will be a cold day in Hell before I sleep with you,' and take into account the fact that I slept with her last night, then number two must be true, and thus I am sure that Hell is exothermic and has already frozen over. The corollary of this theory is that since Hell has frozen over, it follows that it is not accepting any more souls and is therefore, extinct.........leaving only Heaven, thereby proving the existence of a divine being which explains why, last night, Teresa kept shouting 'Oh my God.'"

THIS STUDENT RECEIVED AN A+

## Password

Computer:  Your password has expired.  You must register a new one.

User:  Did anyone discover my password and hack my computer?

Computer:  Your password has expired.  You must get a new one.

User:  Why then do I need a new one as this one seems to be working pretty good?

Computer:  They automatically expire every 30 days.

User:  Can I use the old one and just re-register it?

Computer:  You must get a new one.

User:  I don't want a new one as that is one more thing for me to remember.

Computer:  You must get a new one.

User:  OK, roses

Computer:  You must use more letters.

User: OK! pretty roses

Computer: You must use at least one numeric character.

User: OK!! 1 pretty rose

Computer: You cannot use blank spaces.

User: OK!!! 1prettyrose

Computer: You must use additional characters.

User: OK!!!! 1fuckingprettyrose

Computer: You must use at least one capital letter.

User: OK!!!!! 1FUCKINGprettyrose

Computer: You cannot use more than one capital letter in a row.

User: OK!!!!!! 1Fuckingprettyrose

Computer: You need additional characters.

User: OK!!!!!!!!!!!!

1Fuckingprettyroseshovedupyourassifyoudon'tgivemeaccessrightfuckingnow

Computer: You cannot use that password, as it is already taken.